Things I have to tell you

Things I have to tell you

poems and writing by teenage girls

edited by Betsy Franco

photographs by Nina Nickles

CANDLEWICK PRESS
CAMBRIDGE, MASSACHUSETTS

The author and publisher gratefully acknowledge the following for permission to reprint:
"As Good As She Looks" by Gabrielle Turner first appeared as
"Walking an Invisible Fence" in YO!,* January 30, 1996. "A Man's Strength, But a Woman's Mind"
by Marian Liu first appeared in YO!, November 28, 1995. "A Letter to My Great-Grandmother"
by Sayyadina Denishia Thomas first appeared as "A Letter to My Great-Grandmother She
May Never Read" in YO!, May 14, 1996, under the name Dee Thomas.
"Words" by Mahogany Elaj Foster first appeared in The Secret Life of Words by
Betsy Franco and Maria Damon, Teaching Resource Center, San Diego, 2000.

*YO!, a journal of youth life in the Bay Area, is a project of Pacific News Service.

Library of Congress Cataloging-in-Publication Data
Things I have to tell you: poems and writing by teenage girls / edited by
Betsy Franco ; photographs by Nina Nickles — 1st ed.
p. cm.
Summary: A collection of poems, stories, and essays written by girls fourteen
to nineteen years of age and revealing the secrets which enabled them to overcome
the challenges they faced.
ISBN 0-7636-0905-6 (hardcover). — ISBN 0-7636-1035-6 (paperback)
1. Secrets — Literary collections. 2. Youths' writings. [1. Secrets — Literary collections.
2. Youths' writings.] I. Franco, Betsy. II. Nickles, Nina, ill.

PZ5.S5145 2001
810.8'092837—dc21   99-046884

2 4 6 8 10 9 7 5 3

Printed in Hong Kong
This book was typeset in Gill Sans Light.

Candlewick Press
2067 Massachusetts Avenue
Cambridge, Massachusetts 02140

visit us at www.candlewick.com

Contents

Author's Preface

During my junior high and high school years, I often felt overwhelmed and isolated. Although my friends and I talked about our feelings, the level of sharing was never deep enough for the confusion and pain I was feeling. That period of my life remained vivid, but the idea for *Things I Have to Tell You* didn't surface until Jenna, a friend of mine in her teens, began telling me about some of the experiences she was going through. Listening to her, I felt as though I were reliving my adolescence.

I began to think how valuable it would be to give adolescent girls a way to tell their own stories. I decided to collect poems, stories, and essays by young women twelve to eighteen in order to provide a vehicle for them to communicate their experiences and tell each other how they had made it through some of the challenges in their lives. The purpose of the collection was to give hope, but not at the expense of honesty.

I started in the spring of 1997 by presenting my idea to English and creative writing teachers in the local high schools. My search quickly expanded when I realized it was essential to reach young women from across the country and in different life circumstances. I contacted girls' magazines and organizations, leaders in the field of adolescent development, creative writing journals, and high schools nationwide, including my alma mater.

Visits to my post office box followed. There was almost always something there—a request for guidelines, an offer to help me, and envelopes bulging with manuscripts. Word spread: "My grandmother sent me your guidelines…," "I'm sending this because my creative writing teacher told me…," "I'm mailing this from rehab…," "My brother told me to write…," "My cousin's friend who went to California State Summer School for the Arts said…" By the end, I had received manuscripts by young women from Massachusetts to California, from Canada to Indonesia.

Going to the post office box became a daily ritual. When I read the manuscripts, I cried, I laughed out loud, I talked to myself, I was transformed by the poetry and stories I read. And I was inspired. These young women had something to say. And could they write!

It was very difficult to choose from the forthright, poignant, in-your-face selections I received. As I read and reread the pieces, I talked over my choices with close friends, fellow writers, and teenagers. I felt that each piece was important, that each writer was saying something that needed to be heard. As themes emerged, I found that certain pieces had a timeless quality and an emotional weight that made them stand out.

Finally, after a year and a half, I felt a collection taking shape. I had selected approximately sixty pieces at that point, with a nice mix of poetry and prose. Teen advisers helped me trim it further by offering frank feedback about which pieces would resonate with adolescent girls.

In this final collection, you will find the hope, disillusionment, anger, joy, sadness, and most of all, the strength of young women today. As one author, Marijeta Bozovic, said in one of her submissions, "Women in this decade usually come with a backbone."

Betsy Franco

Photographer's Preface and Acknowledgments

Photographing for *Things I Have to Tell You* has been a wonderful privilege. My goal throughout the process was to remain open to my subjects. The girls I photographed had not read the poems beforehand, nor did I seek to illustrate the poems. The vision of this book from the start has been that, through poetry and through photographs, voices of individual girls would shine through. I didn't pose any of the girls; rather, they let me be the proverbial fly on the wall, often forgetting that I was even there. My days became filled with the after-school and weekend goings-on of teenage girls: we went to the mall, took long walks, went to the swimming pool, hung out, and ate pizzas. I even went to a few parties and proms.

As I watched through my lens, I responded most, I think, to the language, flow, and nuance of gesture—gestures that were at once particular and individual but at the same time expressed so very much. Maybe the photographer Dorothea Lange put it best when she wrote, "Then the camera becomes a beautiful instrument for the purpose of saying to the world in general: 'This is the way it is. Look at it! Look at it!' "

In my search for teenage girls who were willing to have me follow them in their day-to-day life, I met many people who opened doors for me and who opened their hearts to this project. The process has truly been a collaborative effort. Many women are working in their communities on a grassroots level, offering themselves and their ideas to young women. I was fortunate to meet some of those women, and I wish to thank them for their invaluable help and unflagging support: Sister Francis Butler and the entire staff of Mother Caroline Academy in Dorchester, Massachusetts; Elaine DiCicco, principal of the Concord-Carlisle High School; Denise Carver, school psychologist and mentor of the Girls' Forum at the Concord-Carlisle High School; Jean DeCesare; and Mary Orear, founder and director of Mainely Girls.

I especially want to thank the many girls who instinctively understood the meaning of this project and who gave me the opportunity to get to know them: special thanks to Elizabeth Alvarado, Elizabeth Bardeen, Lauren Chartrand, Marian Cooke, Katie Crossman, Amanda Cutaia, Marguerite Delbrun, Michaela Doughty, Angela Duangsay, Alison Dunn, Ana Figueroa, Amanda Finizio, Melissa Fuller, Lindsay Geoghan, Erin Haley, Alison Kuzmickas, Eve Marden, Lauren Maro, Kylah McNeill, Shaucey Nee, Trinity Rackliff, Adelaide Richards, Isabel Richards, Jennifer Rivera, Maritza Rivera, Sarah Slaughter, Elizabeth Theriault, Nydia Valdez, Dolores Vazquez, and Rebecca Wersan. Much thanks to *all* the girls in the sixth, seventh, and eighth grades at Mother Caroline Academy, whom I photographed during the 1998–1999 school year.

Thanks, as well, to Tim Moschini and Alex Aponte.

Heartfelt thanks to my dear friend and editor Mary Lee Donovan, whose vision, sincerity, and dedication have guided the making of this book from the beginning; Senior Designer Anne Moore took a personal interest in the project and was a joy to work with; Associate Editor Kara LaReau offered many wonderful insights. Thanks to Peter Lebovitz and the AGFA Corporation, who provided me with photographic paper. Warm appreciation to my friend and mentor Fred Schreiber, whose gift as a teacher means so much to me.

A special thank-you to my parents, Achilles and Olga Nickles, whose support and love have guided my life. I thank them, too, for my first camera, given to me when I was in high school. I still have that camera; it is with that camera that I began to discover the magic and the joy of looking at the world in a new way. And thank you to my husband, Craig, whose love and kindness exceed words.

Nina Nickles

Things I have to tell you

Secrets

Do you know my secret,
Did I tell you it last night,
Were you listening to my dreams,
Were you hiding out of sight?

Do you look to find my secret,
Reading letters, reading notes,
Picking up sometimes on phone calls,
Opening books to see what I wrote?

Do you really want to know my secret,
Will it answer all your questions,
Take away your mass of worries?
Or maybe, you could ask for my suggestions.

Do you ever think to ask me about my secret,
Being honest and forthright,
With no lies or hidden feelings?
Only then will my secret come to light.

◆

Jessica L. McCloskey, age 16

as a child i was taught that women were, by nature, gentle creatures.

considering this, i looked in

the st. martin's roget's thesaurus, at the listing for gentle:

moderate, nonviolent, reasonable, judicious, *tame, mild as milk,* innocuous,

innocent, *weak,* RESTRICTED, LIMITED, *chastened,* subdued, calm, still,

untroubled, peaceable, PINK, nonextreme, indifferent, soft, NOT TOUGH,

tender, yielding, compressible, padded, BROKEN, BROKEN IN, *docile,*

domestic, MUTED, inaudible, *feeble,* unemphatic, HUSHED, *dull, dead,*

STIFLED, lax, loose, infirm, *crippled,* undemanding, *weak-willed, weak-kneed,*

unmasterful, LACKING AUTHORITY, uninfluential, lenient,

LONG-SUFFERING, *merciful,* unexcitable, cold, *frigid, heavy,* deadpan,

good-tempered, sunny, demure, reserved, lamblike, meek, unambitious, amiable,

nice, sweet, sociable, SERVILE, HARMLESS, *well-behaved, obedient,*

benevolent, CHRISTIAN, affectionate, charitable, pure, immaculate, white,

uncorrupted, undefiled, unfallen, *sinless,* KNOWING

NO BETTER, *dovelike, angelic.*

out of curiosity, i checked *woman.*

under *spinster,* i saw—

new woman, career woman, suffragette,

then: wench, nymph, burd, filly, blonde, brunette, platinum blonde, sweetheart,

moll, doll, BIT OF FLUFF, mistress, courtesan, shrew, amazon.

oh, my.

sigh.

◆

Idit Meltzer Agam, age 15

My Heart Is in My Throat

Excuse me while I clear my throat—
I might pause with uncertainty
and turn a little red,
but please remain seated,
     I'll be with you soon.

Excuse me while I clear my throat—
you may hear a few squeaks and cracks,
and see me shake uncontrollably,
but please remain seated,
     I'll be with you soon.

Excuse me while I clear my throat—
I may close my eyes and look
invisible, but I am still here with you.
I have never done this before,
I have never sung a song
my song
of inner   hopes   and   fears.
They may seem silly, childish, inscrutable,
and may take me a minute,   year
but please remain seated,
     I'll be with you soon.

◆

Erin B. Henry, age 17

I'm Sayin'

Yo!

I would be a liar

If I was to say I didn't care about all of the madness

The destruction.

I mean sure I think about the future of my peers

And all of the *younguns*

I think about the lies that have been fed to them

And I think about all the ones who just sat there and ate it all up.

MMM, man *I'm sayin'!*

Why spend up all of your time abiding by social rules?

Why spend up all of your time following trends and fads?

Why spend up all your time thinking about what people are thinking about you?

Why try to appeal to the masses?

Why not go out on a limb and be who you want to be?

What if one day you decided to wear your hair nappy?

Sport your tribal colors?

Throw up your fists?

Quote Malcolm X and Martin Luther King,
Read Nikki Giovanni and Angela Davis,
Dance the dance of *Mother* Africa,
Greet people in Swahili!
Be STRONG and PROUD,
While being honest and *trusting*,
And *Hard-working*.
Yo! Is there a way?
Is there a way?
Man . . . I'm Sayin'!

◆

Mahogany Elaj Foster, age 16

Escape

I look inside me and I don't see it
I don't see the power
The confidence you say I have
You say I can do anything
That I'm sure of myself and my intentions
And I wonder
But I don't know
If it's all there
Waiting for the opportunity
to jump into you
And try to help you
Fix you
Ask you
Why? Because I don't know
I wait anxiously
Feeling my stomach
A block of ice
Chipping away, melting,
then freezing up again
Who can I follow?
Cuz I don't want to lead
I ask myself every question

There are temporary answers
But I know more
Like everybody seems to know more
And I still don't know how
Cuz it's nice to ignore confrontation
Avoid conflict
Watch my rainbow
And let you watch yours
But the universe knows more
I must take this test just like everyone
Takes tests
I am closing in on the sky
Hoping it will try to escape
And I know I will let it get away
Like I let a lot of things get away
Cuz then I won't have to continue the
search
For my power

◆

Theresa Hossfeld, age 16

A Girl Snapping
or My Application for Advanced Placement English

educator - n. one who or that which educates

education - n. the act or process of imparting knowledge, developing the powers of reasoning and judgment, and generally of preparing intellectually for mature life

Sometimes I'm tempted to sue the school system for my parents' tax money. However, the actual cash would go to my parents, and they have too much money as it is.

English should have been my favorite subject. I ought to have had teachers that could make me cry in class. Each day should have meant an opportunity to learn something, share something, and receive feedback I could respect. In spite of the school system, I have so far managed to maintain a burning interest in literature and related fields. (Look up **disillusionment, self-education,** and **renewed faith.**)

Advanced Placement English is described as challenging, inspiring, and intense. I say, finally. It is a trifle ironic that the students have to write applications to be accepted—I think the department should write us an application and prove that the class will be up to our standards. Let's see if the high school can offer me an English class that will make me sweat. Then I'll be willing to rethink my criticism. Otherwise, I'll be back to my usual hobby of picking through the trash in hopes of finding the Holy Grail.

◆

Marijeta Bozovic, age 16

New Honesty

Today I gave up
a promising career of "truth."
Profound state of love
stepped in like a puzzle piece.
Completing, no, not
the Empire State Building,
not Mt. Rushmore or
van Gogh's *Sunflowers*.
Completing instead
my departure from "honesty."
Can I find a balance
between me and
the box I call my family?
I want equilibrium.
I want subtle change.
I want to tell the Truth,
not the truth of the woman
who snapped on a collar
and named me alive.

Like a plastic ball,
I toss between myself
and the various identities
I have been assigned.
Look out—I fell in the mud.
Look out—I opened my mouth,
and out came ideas
you don't think are pretty.
I suppose it would be scary
to be a ventriloquist who found out
her dummy can talk,
to find the doll had a brain
and opinions that will bite
when provoked.
I suppose it would be scary
if I opened my coat
and showed you all my secrets.
Would you call me a flasher
and file charges?

Would you gaze blindly
refusing to see the Truth?
I'm sorry to tell you
that I'm not sorry anymore.
I can only run for so long
and so far.
I'm done,
and I'm throwing up my Truth
like a marathon runner
at the end
of a 16-year race.

◆

Jessie Childress, age 16

Hallway Between Lunch and English
(Freud Can Kiss My Sexually Ambiguous Arse)

we all like to strut
(squeak of black boots on yellow linoleum)
and show our teeth
in primitive smiles
(crack of bubble gum
like the sound of a slamming locker)
we put on our chatter
like red lipstick
with the same amount
of greasy enthusiasm
all our secret glances are pulled on
like a fishnet stocking over white thigh
oh the brittle irony
slips out

like smoke pouring from sultry lips
we are all armed
with our polysyllabic sabers
uniformed by our lust
united by our laughter
unique by our will
we march together toward
the war we cannot name
but at least we are dressed for it

◆

Danya Goodman, age 15

Be Perfect
Perfect brain
Perfect personality
Perfect face
Perfect body
Perfect body
Perfect body
—Shocking studies show eating disorders
   on the rise in teenage girls—
Shocking
Bullshit
You should have seen this coming
You raised me
Your society screwed me up
I read your hypocritical magazines
I went to your schools
I dealt with your sons' running commentaries
on
my face
my weight
my breasts
my body
Shocking
Bullshit

My parents can't protect me
My friends can't protect me
My wonderful, loving,
ignorant community can't protect me
So I protect them
I have to cope to survive
Why hurt them too?
        What?
        Oh, I'm fine, Mom
        ~ smile ~
Be Perfect
Bullshit
◆

Laura Veuve, age 15

Finding Joy

I found myself a place
to be, to play
a day went by or maybe two
no thoughts of you to crowd my empty mind
I find my body is to me
as lovely as
a budding tree
a cat with grace
and emerald eyes
so unconcerned with shapely thighs
just me
Invisibly
a girl
inside this shape
a woman's hips and breasts
so much wider, softer than the rest
I found myself a crystal blue
like nymphs or faeries do

I never thought of you
or what you'd think of me
I found my body was
a mass of ground
the earth inside of me
behind my vinyl walls of
picture perfection
I was the earth, the sky
it made me want to cry
to shout the softness
I have never dared let out
my curves, my hair
a part of who I was
a blonde in a clear glass pond
myself a flow of nature
alone
finding joy
◆

Marissa Korbel, age 16

As Good As She Looks

When I look at the television, I see images of women too beautiful to touch. At the other end of the spectrum I see the women of my own culture, the women I grew up with. This woman does not look dainty or feminine, but has the signs of hard work and worry etched on her face. I am in love with the image of the strong woman who takes care of her own.

But everywhere I turn I hear that a woman is only as good as she looks. Everywhere I turn I see more young girls hurting or even killing themselves in an effort to starve themselves into the "ideal" woman.

I want to run back to the safety of my own culture—a culture where strong women are revered and appreciated. But this culture is disappearing as it gives in to the American ideal. No longer is the African American woman with the few extra pounds considered a pretty lady—now she's seen as lazy and ignorant. Even a culture that used to pride itself on its full-hipped women can fall victim to the American idea of skin and bones.

The sad thing is, I don't know how to resolve this in my own life. I can rant and rave all day about the oppressed women, but at the end of the day, people will still judge me. And I will keep trying to change myself to fit their standards.

By focusing on how women look instead of how we feel and think, society silences our voices. By making us objects of beauty, it takes away our spirits and our souls.

◆

Gabrielle Turner, age 19

Contemplating fat and thin
as I lift my foot upon the scale
my heart skips a beat
to see the torturous needle
point to the number I don't want to see
No food, you're fat
double the run
I want this day to end
I step upon the scale that night
to see the number low
A smile stretches across my face
my heart skips a beat
I open my eyes to see
the scale at just eye level
a bruise from just the night before
and one today to match that one
from tumbling to the floor
Contemplating fat and thin
Never enough
It feels like I will never win.

◆

Becky Mann, age 17

Damn, I Look Good

Tried on a dress the other day,
Showed off my skin
In just the right way,
Rolled off my hips
Like fingertips,
Legs long,
Heart strong,
Cascading hair falling
Just to where my back
Lies graceful, smooth, bare.
Elegant shoulders,
Slender wrist,
Temptress in a dress
No one can resist.
Supercilious walk,

Suave talk,
This coquette can get
Any man she's set
Eyes upon—
A female Don Juan.
The best, I confess,
Cannot help but obsess
Over me,
Devil walking
In one hell of a dress.

◆

Miriam Stone, age 16

A Man's Strength, But a Woman's Mind

An explosion rattles behind Ranma's swift steps. He is still stuck as a girl—there's no water close by to change him back to his original form. As long as he has to be a girl, Ranma decides, he might as well be the best girl he can be. He can still punch out all the bad guys while keeping his girlish figure.

I am not a superhero who changes gender by touching water, nor do I punch out bad guys on a daily basis. But like Ranma, in this Japanese *anime*, I break the stereotype of a girl as a dainty little thing who needs a man by her side in order to do anything. Like Ranma, I try to be the best girl that I can be.

But no matter how far women reach in sports, the job market, or school, we still cannot walk down the street at night without the fear of some man coming from the shadows and raping us. No matter how many self-defense classes we take, no matter how much pepper spray we carry, there is always that insecurity. That's what I hate most about being female.

My mom is stuck in another female trap—that of the little wife who is confined to the kitchen, following her husband's bidding. She had to give up a career as a dentist to follow Chinese tradition, where the husband is "king" and the wife is beneath the children. I've decided that if someone won't treat me as an equal, then I won't marry him. I told my mother about my feelings the other day, and she answered, "I used to think like that too, but then I got married and had kids." But I won't let marriage destroy my hopes and dreams.

Nor will I succumb to society's efforts to confine me: high heels that oppose the law of gravity, miniskirts that limit the length of my steps, miracle bras to boost my breasts, special jeans to make my rear higher. I prefer T-shirts and athletic sandals.

My grandfather gave me the name Ming—a male name meaning "bright." The character is made up of the moon and the sun: two conflicting entities. He named me this to give me strength—the strength not to be a typical female.

◆

Marian Liu, age 17

Anime is Japanese animation.

Tall Single ISO Coffee

All I wanted was a cup of coffee
but when I asked for
"a tall single, please"
the guy at the coffee stand
thought I was asking for him.
I suppose
I look like a tall single
and maybe he thought
that I was looking for a tall single
but believe me,
I only wanted a drink.
Something tall enough
to wake me up,
not too strong,
just tall . . . and single.
Even if I didn't want coffee
and I was looking for some tall single
it would be a girl
some tall single girl
with brown eyes
and a tough walk

who wrote poetry
like the world was ending.
Even if I didn't have a girlfriend
with all of the above,
including the tough walk,
I wouldn't want this coffee boy.
Even though he is
tall & single
What he can't comprehend
is that I didn't stop
and give him a second look.
Quite frankly,
I don't care
if he is tall and single.
I just want to see my girlfriend
and I want some coffee.

◆

Anonymous, age 16

ISO—in search of

I am stuck inside this cocoon. I hear the leaves dropping to the ground from the inside. You ask me if I am a virgin? A virgin to what? A virgin to heartbreak? no. A virgin to being another version? no. A virgin to being fucked, and left without confidence, and an empty bed the next morning? Well, yes . . .

I have this gift, they so lovingly like to put it. I haven't met the right guy, yeah that's the ticket. I haven't found the right place, or the right time. He did say, "I will love you forever," didn't he? Well girl, I guess forever ended, or never began.

◆

Julia Gillam, age 15

Apricot Bath

I don't want to be sexy right now
I don't feel like arranging myself
in positions that will delight your eyes
Arranging myself so that my stomach doesn't show
so that you can't see my feet
I don't feel like making the effort
I want to sit next to you
in an apricot bubble bath
and talk about why your politics conflict with mine
without your staring at my breasts
I want to sit cross-legged
lean forward with my elbows on my knees
and listen to your reasoning
without your peering down between my thighs
I want us to be two sexless beings
Watching the steam curl off the water

But if you must love me
Love the little smooth scar on my knee
not my eyes
Love my round belly
not my legs
Love the two freckles on my neck
that look like a vampire's kiss
not my lips
Love my square, pudgy toes
not my smile
I want to inhale the apricot fumes
brush the bubbles from your shoulder
and argue with you over our beliefs
I don't want anything to be sexual
even though we're both naked and
our feet are kissing under the tepid water
I want us to stay in the bath
until we don't know
where water ends and skin begins
Until I know
why you are who you are
Until you love me
for my flaws and what I believe in

Then we can rise from the water
skin soft and glowing
like apricots, lit from within
wrap ourselves in the towels
of each other and then
you can kiss me

◆

Lindsay Henry, age 17

31

Nudity
Lying together on the purple floor
exposed to the fullest extent
for a moment in time

Indecent
is how I begin to see myself
I begin building up my walls again
brick by brick, but quickly
To be naked is to be vulnerable

Conformity
is growing back
like a dandelion pulled up
but with roots still deep in the ground
I put flowers on Individuality's grave
not entirely sad
the nervousness is fading
the purple fades to mist

Unmasked
but not for long
I look for my shield
and find my mask under the bed
I slip it on; it's warm and secure
but still a little uncomfortable

She is not quite dressed
but she is hurrying to cover up
she exposed herself too much tonight
she feels dirty
she is, and so am I
but my walls are cleansing

We are no longer ashamed
We stare at each other
through identical masks of invincibility
while we hide inside
and smile in relief

◆

Greta, age 14

A Bad Hair Day

The day I met you was a bad hair day.
This one piece of hair
Just wouldn't stay!

You must have noticed,
You must have seen,
Because although you weren't rude,
And although you weren't mean,

You were just a little distant,
Your mind in another place,
You weren't interested in me,
I could see it in your face.

So after a handshake,
A talk for a while,
You excused yourself
With a pleasant smile.

But what would have happened
If my hair had looked good,
If it wasn't sticking up,
Had stayed down like it should?

Would we have talked longer?
Would you have flirted more?
Asked me to a movie
As you walked me to the door?

Maybe we would date,
You would give me a ring.
Soon we'd be married,
Have kids, the whole thing!

Or maybe we would just
Have shared a night of fun.
But it could have been love.
You could have been the one.

But instead you turned away,
Moved on to another girl,
And again we were two strangers
Floating in this world.

It's scary to me
That my future could lay
On one piece of hair
That just wouldn't stay.

◆

Miriam Stone, age 15

Just Another Girl?

You told me I was beautiful,
and it made me smile . . .
            like a little girl.
I wanted you to want me.
I wanted you to love me . . .
            like a woman.
You kissed me and my mind felt secure.
You held me and my heart felt warm . . .
            and my eyes were closed.
You opened me up
and took what you needed . . .
            and I let you.

When you kissed me good-bye,
I smelled my scent on your face.
When you walked out the door,
I stared at the back of your head
as it grew smaller and farther away . . .
            and disappeared.

You left me with nothing but a taste in
my mouth.
You left me alone with a ten-minute memory.
You left me.

You never saw the tears.
They were dry long before you came back.
I opened my eyes and saw right through you.

Now I smile without you . . .
            Now I am a woman.

◆

Cindy Lisica, age 18

Get Yourself Another Dog

The humane society tells people that there's no use trying to train a biting dog not to bite. It is in his nature and there is nothing anyone can do. The humane society says you just have to put him to sleep and find yourself another dog.

◆

Marijeta Bozovic, age 16

It's not the size that counts

My hair blows in the wind, because it is growing regrets.
My eyes slant because I'm laughing, laughing at you.
My fists clench because I'm ready to fight, ready to fight you.
My shoulders are small, yet big enough to shrug you off.
My feet are tiny, yet big enough to walk away from you.
My hands are small, yet big enough to wave good-bye to you.
Smoke is coming from my mouth, because the fire in my heart for you is out.
[written in chemistry]

◆

Julia Gillam, age 14

Clouds Rolling In

my friend and i
got caught in a storm
with tears for rain,
and shouts for thunder,
lightning fists
lashing out.
i pause,
puzzled.
we fight all the time,
don't know why.
i want to ask
but am afraid of the reason.
it's my fault
(always is).
he says so.
he's never wrong.
uses this weather to prove it.

i am afraid of lightning.
don't let it strike me again
again
again
i am the sun
that these black clouds cover up.
why won't they go away
and let me shine for once?

i'm afraid of storms.

◆

Melissa Leigh Davis, age 14

The Consequence of Loving Me

He thought he knew me,
so he touched my throat,
expecting a kiss.
But I whisked him away
like an apple off a tree,
the consequence
of loving me.

He thought I cared,
so he shared
his deepest creepy secret.
In my head it mushroomed
into a balloon
and then it popped—
the secret was set free,
the consequence
of loving me.

He thought he could change
my bitchy, witchy ways.
He thought I'd listen to him whisper
when he said I was a blister.

But instead I sang him off
with my snitchy melody,
the consequence
of loving me.

My lesson to you
if you think I am sweet
and you want to meet me,
don't,
because I stab backs
and I never relax
until the climax
where I hit
you, tittering in shock.
The happiness you wish
will never really be
the consequence
of loving me.

◆

Carli Taylor, age 14

My Ode to Crank

Rolling smoke-foggy glass
Hit it slow—so you'll go fast
In awe you watch it crystallize
A miracle before your eyes
Light the fire, turn it slow
Watch the rock start to go
Its beauty makes your heart beat quick
Your love is thriving in a glass dick
The taste and smell is ecstasy
A line or two will set you free
Your heart and mind begin to race
You feel a smile form on your face

Your pain and worries are all gone
But somehow you know it's wrong
Your love for crank has grown so strong
But you know this feeling can't last long
You'll need a line or another bowl
You'll depend on it to fill the hole
That has become so big inside
From the truth you cannot hide
The drug you loved so through and through
Has no feelings back for you

◆

Lisa Woodward, age 15

Born at 15

A childhood of
    repeated molestations,
    suffocation by drugs,
    tragedy replacing hopscotch,
I grew crooked in the sunlight.

A smart kid,
    "teacher's pet"
    whom no boys liked,
    tall, socially inept, and awkward,
I broke my own heart so many times.

A teenager,
    backward but witty,
    someone stopped
    to look at me.
I fell in love with a horrible person.

A year lost spinning on drugs,
    drowning in tears, burned in loud music.
    A disease had forced himself
    into more than my physicality.

Balled up in a corner, tasting salt,
I went numb while he read a magazine.

I took a mountain vacation,
    wet green health soothed
    my swollen eyes,
I met a broad, scarred man, never without his bicycle.

I watched the white gold moon over a mountain,
    the black tree outline trying
    to hide it, my soul, from me.
    I talked to myself pretending
    it was to the man next to me,
    about past and present
    about my horrible fearful future.
I realized I had given all my power
    to the things I hated.

A warm, fluid feeling
    rushed inside my spirit,
    so unusual.
It must have been myself being born.

◆

Melissa Parker, age 16

Afraid

Do you hear the voices
floating through the wind
following me,
they laugh and whisper
as I turn and my hair blows forward
attempting to shield my face.
I've yet to realize
they can't chase me
if I don't run from them.

◆

Cindy Lisica, age 16

A Letter to My Great-Grandmother

Dear Mama,

I love you for deciding I would be your child. At sixty-nine years of age, you had already sired one generation and I was two generations down and illegitimate. You fed me when I cried. You dealt with my toddler years and those incessant questions. You combed my hair and tried to prepare my young mind and soul for the complications you knew couldn't be avoided. You read to me every day and opened my mind to my history, made me stand against the wall for half an hour every other day so my back would be straight.

Oh, and I remember walking with you to the Red Cross, when you were seventy-four and I was five years old, to collect that salty government cheese and butter, that canned fruit and bread. So I could eat well, which I did, and you would not let me touch any pork. You made some fried chicken to die for, and Mama, thank you for that bread pudding and for never asking where I got the pumpkin on Halloween.

Thank you for discipline and for old stories about the South where the blood relatives are. I love you, Mama, for giving me a sense of character. Thank you for being happy I am a girl and teaching me pride in being a woman of color, helping to find where my roots are, and always telling me I was intelligent

and just as good if not karmically cleaner than those who seemed
to get more chances than me. You told me to get in touch with all
cultural sides in myself and that they all had many things in common
and I was merged and complete.

Mama, do you remember when I asked to be a Black Panther
for Halloween and you told me I was a Black Panther every day in
your house. Then you proceeded to tell me about The Cause, and
about everyone from the Queen of Sheba to Malcolm X. Then when
you started to get senile from life's stresses finally catching up to you,
I know you tried to send me to relatives, tried to keep me out of
the system, away from foster care and residential treatment houses.
When it didn't work, you did everything you could, riding the bus
for an hour to visit me in a group house when you were eighty-one.

Now you'll be eighty-five next month. I know there have been
times when your love has been almost all I've had. You done been
through it, Mama, and I give you every iota of respect in my soul.
It ain't enough, in my opinion, though you don't seem to ask for
even that much. You just want to see me on the right mental and
moral track.

I love you for that, Mama, and I always will. You got to be the
biggest player I know. Telling me when I'm making you proud and
loving me with no strings attached.

◆

Sayyadina Denishia M. Thomas, age 14

Song for a Girl

This is a song
for a sixth-grade girl
who, after trying
to kill herself
once a month
for six months,
has failed.
The marks, burns, cuts
are beginning to fade,
as they do
after three weeks' time.
She still wears long sleeves.
She still lets her hair hang
over her neck.
Her body is trying to forget,
scar tissue is forming,
her liver is trying
to rid itself of the aspirin
she breathed in like air
in hopes of making herself stop
breathing.

This is a song
for a sixth-grade girl
who, like myself,
has failed.
We carry the failure with us
everywhere we go,
like an organ donor card.
Our thoughts are consumed
by this failure.
It haunts us,
unfinished and twitching.
At night the corpse of this urge
struggles to stand,
tries to convince us,
squirms through the cracks
in our head.
It kicks our walls and
in the morning we find
bruises we don't remember getting
or giving.

This is a song
for the pattern that began long ago,
that ate us alive
until we finally got the hang of it,
learned how to cut our skin,
learned how to hate ourselves
like so many others.
It took us years
but we finally figured it out.
And once we knew,
it became all we knew.
Pain was our best friend,
it was our lover,
it was the only thing
that we would trust.
We became dependent,
couldn't make it through
a day without our pain.
When we tried to stop cutting ourselves,
our skin ached.
It demanded our attention
and pain was the only attention
we knew how to give.

This is a song
of recognition.
We have learned to recognize
the urge as a part of us.
It has grown with us
through the years.
It has changed and
grown on its own as well.
It is in my body
no less than my heart.
It is a part of my existence
no less than my soul.
It is ancient,
burning through my body,
and I have learned
to find a peace in it.
A home.

This is a song
because we cry without
explanation
because we are two beings
because we shift
in our desires and moods
like the winds.

This is a song
for uncertainty,
for the way we wake each morning
hoping that we won't
lose control that day and
end up walking through our days
only out of respect for habits.
Hoping we will learn to let out
the yelling fighting
screaming crying hating
howling that's caught in our heads
so our insides can match
the images we project.

This is a song
for that fight,
a perpetual struggle
between honesty and composure,
between realness and masks,
a perpetual struggle
to bring our split lives
back into one.

This is a song
and I'm trying to sing it.
I'm hoping this song will help me
loosen the grip of these patterns.
This is a song
and I want to give it to
the sixth-grade girl
who's failed
time and time again
as I have.
I want this song
to convince us both that
our failure to die
might be okay.

I want this song
to be a shield
between now and the next time
the urge takes over.
I want this song
to save the girl I don't know.
I want this song
to save myself.

◆

Jessie Childress, age 16

54

Words

Words fly across the paper like blackbirds across the sky

and I think to myself why oh

why oh why

why why,

Why would anyone use words like

I hate and

I can't and

I quit therefore I won't and

Goodbye.

Good bye?

Why not take that beautiful skill and use words like

I love and

I can and

I will or

at least I'll try and

Hello . . . hello,

because I believe in word conservation

and if you're going to use a word at all

it should be one that glides off of your tongue

and floats around to sit comfortably in someone's ear.
So the next time I see you
I'll be using words like
I love and
I can and
I will or
at least I'll try and
Hello . . . hello.
Yeah, words.

◆

Mahogany Elaj Foster, age 16

To Live

I sit in my
crunched-in
restraining
desk, they call it,
with my paper
and my pen
and I am
supposed to see
the blackboard
around the tall boy
en frente de mi
and my mind on my
text and my pen on
the page I am
supposed to
for me
para mi futuro.
but my head
won't translate
this language
log base b of a squared
carbon monoxide

reacting with phosphorus
I don't react
I see through the paper
and my pen writes
poetic equations
my mind plus my life
equals
something beyond this.
doodles litter my
notebook like snowflakes
dancing through the trees
beyond the window
the lined paper
lines with soul
forgetting cosines
life without phosphorus
and my life
mi futuro
beyond desk-chairs
And dull muraled halls
j.v., varsity and
setting the curve
school play and G.P.A.
textbooks

learning without
knowing
without room
to learn how
to know myself
to be myself
trial and error
minus lab write-up
feeling without
a thesis
learning youth
mi futuro
learning how to live
without a textbook
without a teacher to
correct grammar
to live to learn myself
to live to know myself
to live to be somebody
who's learned how
to live

◆

Miriam Stone, age 16

58

I know I am strong
  both in my convictions and in myself.
I know I am beautiful
  both inside and out.
I know I am powerful
  and growing more so.
I know I will do just fine.

◆

Laura Veuve, age 15

Author's Acknowledgments

This collection is not only about the selections in it. Many people were involved at each stage of the book, some of whom I knew and many of whom worked behind the scenes.

Thomas Schellenberg, my son's high school creative writing teacher at Palo Alto High School, honored the project from the start. Jennifer Abrams invited me to her "Women Writers" class at Gunn High School and allowed me to introduce my idea to her students. In the same classroom, poets MaryLee McNeil and Nancy Mohr let me sit in on their poetry workshops.

When I wrote to Mary Pipher, the author of *Reviving Ophelia: Saving the Selves of Adolescent Girls*, she offered helpful suggestions and an encouraging handwritten message that I immediately posted on my wall: "Let's change the world together."

Ads in *Poets and Writers Magazine, Moon Magazine,* and with the Girls, Inc. organization enabled me to reach a national audience. Kim Whiting and D. K. Bihler at *empowered, the magazine for young females*, gave me a long list of writers to contact. Joseph McCarren, who heads Slippery Rock University's summer program, helped me contact many strong writers. Nell Bernstein from *YO!* in San Francisco, and her assistant, Michelle Koukhab, generously took the time to help me select works from a diverse group of writers. In a serendipitous moment, I discovered that John Fox, author of *Poetic Medicine: The Healing Art of Poem-Making,* had a post office box near mine, and he ended up giving me support throughout the project.

Very special thanks to Lorraine Noyes, a writer, who acted as one of my consultants. She was deeply dedicated to the book, and lent her special brand of wisdom to each stage of the process. Thank you as well to Maria Damon, a writer and literature professor at the University of Minnesota, who supported me wholeheartedly as a consultant. Both Lorraine and Maria kept me going when I lost sight of my purpose.

A poem by Laura Veuve inspired the title of the book. My teen advisers—Jenni Brown, Jenna Elinor, Jessica Hebert, Siena Kautz, and Casey Weiss—read all of the initial selections and gave me invaluable feedback. In the editing stage, Marjorie Franco provided assistance.

My agent, Amy Rennert, helped me in every way through the final stretch. Mary Lee Donovan, my editor at Candlewick, had the sensitivity and passion necessary to make the collection work as a whole. Associate Editor Kara LaReau was dedicated to the book. Throughout the project my husband, Douglas, and my sons, James, Thomas, and David, were behind me.

Finally, I wish to thank all the young women who shared their experiences, whether or not their work made it into this collection.

Betsy Franco